We Don't Want
To March Straight

We Don't Want To March Straight

Masculinity, Queers and the Military

Peter Tatchell

CASSELL

**Other titles in the Listen Up! series
in the Cassell Sexual Politics list include:**

Cassell plc
Wellington House
125 Strand
London
WC2R 0BB

215 Park Avenue South
New York
NY 10003

First published 1995

British Library Cataloguing-in-Publication Data
A catalogue record for this book is
available from the British Library.

ISBN: 0-304-33373-5

Design and typesetting by
Ben Cracknell
Printed and bound in Great Britain by
Biddles Ltd, Guildford and Kings Lynn

Contents

Dedication

For Harry Hay and Pat Arrowsmith and in honour of all queers everywhere who refuse to conform to the machismo of straight male culture and militarism.

Acknowledgements

We Don't *Want To March Straight* reworks ideas that have been recurrent themes in much of my writing and activism over the last 26 years. The arguments concerning the anti-democratic character of the military, and its role in the suppression of freedom, develop from my own earlier *Democratic Defence*, published in 1985 with the much-appreciated encouragement of David Fernbach at GMP. I am also greatly indebted to my queer activist comrades in OutRage!. And to Steve Cook at Cassell for many discussions that have helped sharpen my ideas.

Above all, much of the inspiration for this book is owed to the American queer emancipationist and anti-militarist, Harry Hay, who founded the modern movement for lesbian and gay human rights in 1950, and to the British lesbian peace activist, Pat Arrowsmith, who has been for 40 years at the forefront of the campaigns for nuclear disarmament, colonial freedom and British withdrawal from the north of Ireland.

Peter Tatchell, London, May 1995.

About The Author

Peter Tatchell was born in Melbourne, Australia, in 1952. Opposed to United States and Australian aggression against the people of Vietnam, in the late 1960s he became active in the National Campaign Against Conscription, the Draft Resister's Union, Christians For Peace and the Vietnam Moratorium Campaign, helping to organize the huge Stop Work To Stop The War demonstrations which immobilized Melbourne in 1970.

Unwilling to be drafted into a genocidal war, and faced with the alternative of two years imprisonment, Peter Tatchell went into exile in London in 1971. Five days after his arrival, he joined the newly-formed Gay Liberation Front and, a little later, the Troops Out Movement, supporting its campaign for an end to the British military occupation of north-east Ireland. Since 1971, he has been involved in nearly every major campaign for homosexual human rights in Britain.

After completing college, Peter Tatchell began working as a journalist, specializing in undercover investigative reporting. In 1978, to gather material for a book exposing the class-ridden, anti-democratic and imperialistic culture of the British armed forces, he applied for an officer's commission in the Royal Artillery, participated in training exercises in artillery and tank warfare, and was offered a place at the Royal Military Academy Sandhurst (which he declined).

On the basis of these experiences and subsequent research, he wrote *Democratic Defence: A Non-Nuclear Alternative* (GMP, London, 1985). Arguing for the armed forces to be de-imperialized, this book expounded the themes of non-nuclear and non-provocative defence, civil rights for military personnel, community-based citizen's armies, and non-violent civilian resistance.

During the 1980s, Peter Tatchell lectured at the Royal Military Academy Sandhurst, the Army Staff College Camberley, the Royal Naval College Greenwich and the Royal

College of Defence Studies Belgravia. His military theories of defensive defence have been the subject of dissertations by officers at Sandhurst and Camberley.

In 1983 he stood unsuccessfully as the Labour candidate in the Bermondsey by-election. Pilloried for his socialist convictions, refusal to fight in Vietnam, advocacy of lesbian and gay human rights, and his opposition to the wars in the north of Ireland and the Falklands, he was subject to more media slurs and violent assaults than any other political candidate in Britain this century.

There were demands in 1985 for Peter Tatchell to be charged with sedition and incitement to mutiny following his television and leaflet appeal for military personnel to refuse orders for the preparation and use of nuclear weapons of mass destruction.

A leading activist in the radical direct action group OutRage! since 1990, Peter Tatchell is Britain's most prominent theorist and campaigner for queer emancipation. Vilified and demonized by right-wing newspapers and politicians as a "traitor", "extremist" and "subversive", he has been placed under police surveillance, blacklisted by the Economic League, threatened with assassination by neo-Nazis and subject to hundreds of personal assaults and attacks on his home. He nevertheless remains a defiant, outspoken voice for queer freedom. His recent books include *Europe In The Pink: Lesbian & Gay Equality in the New Europe* (GMP, London, 1992) and *Safer Sexy: The Guide to Gay Sex Safely* (Freedom Editions, London, 1994).

one

Gay Liberation Versus Militarism

"Homosexuals should not fight in a war propagated by a society that fucks us over in all its institutions. We will not fight in an army that discriminates against us".

These words, written in the San Francisco Free Press in the shadow of the Stonewall Riots of 1969, called on lesbians and gay men to refuse military service in the defence of straight society. They were echoed by the emergent lesbian and gay liberation movement which urged total rejection of the "insane war in Vietnam" and an end to "complicity in the war". "We oppose any attempts by the movement to obtain security clearances for homosexuals since they contribute to the war machine", declared the Youth Committee of the North American Conference of Homophile Organizations in August 1969.

In November that year, the massive Moratorium Against The War march in San Francisco was joined by thousands of lesbians and gay men chanting "One-two-three-four, we don't want your macho war", some carrying placards reading "SUCK COCK TO BEAT THE DRAFT".

A quarter of a century later, attitudes towards the armed forces are very different. The US lesbian and gay movement now has its own patriotic, flag-waving organization, the Campaign For Military Service. As its name suggests, it has an agenda which goes beyond mere opposition to homophobia in the armed forces. It is *in favour of* service in the military, positively endorsing that institution's values and objectives. To the theme tune of 'God Bless America', the Campaign demands for homosexuals the "right to serve" in the US army that in 1965 invaded the Dominican Republic to sustain a fascist dictatorship and in 1968 massacred the villagers of My Lai in Vietnam.

Even mainstream lesbian and gay rights groups have enthusiastically embraced the right-to-serve agenda, emphasizing the star-spangled loyalty of homosexuals to 'the American way'. No equality campaign is now complete without a line-up of clean-cut, all-American gay servicemen and women who eagerly swear the oath of allegiance and sing the national anthem. Indeed, homosexual soldiers and war veterans, many of them uniformed and sporting campaign ribbons, were the centrepiece of the 1993 March On Washington For Lesbian, Gay & Bisexual Rights.

This shift to an implicitly pro-military stance is not confined to the US. In Britain, at the behest of the lesbian and gay lobbying organization, the Stonewall Group, the 1993 Lesbian & Gay Pride march in London featured uniformed and bemedalled veterans, including Americans who had served in the US army during the Vietnam era and English who had waged war in Ireland.

In their new-found enthusiasm to defend the right of queers to bear arms, none of the major lesbian and gay rights groups question whether or not the military is a worthy and honourable institution, and whether or not queers should take part in a homophobic organization that has so frequently been involved in gross violations of human rights. Even the modest aim of reforming the military, to make it democratic and prevent its use as an instrument of oppression, does not figure on the agenda of the mainstream lesbian and gay organizations.

What a turn-around. A movement which began in 1969 with the aim of changing society now seeks conformity with the straight status quo. Instead of social transformation, it aspires to assimilation. The narrow and limited goal of equal rights, and reformist *realpolitik*, have supplanted the idealism of gay liberation. Devoid of vision, much of the contemporary gay rights agenda is about queers adapting to hetero society. Any dissent from the ethics of straight institutions, like the military, is deferred for the sake of shortterm political expediency.

The homophobia of the armed forces is indefensible and should of course be opposed. There can be no justification for arbitarily excluding people from any job, including the military, because of their sexual orientation. However, much of the gay rights movement now goes far beyond merely opposing discrimination to defend 'the right' to military service, and suggest that 'serving one's country' is a worthwhile aspiration for queers. This lends legitimacy to the armed forces and all they stand for.

Implicit in the campaign for the right to serve in the military is the assumption that all the rights that straights have are desirable and that queers should have them too, including the right to wage war and kill other human beings. It abandons any critical assessment of the institutions of heterosexual society in favour of a wholly uncritical, even slavish, worship of all things straight. This mentality, whereby queers mimic the worst aspects of hetero culture, is the height of self-disrespect.

The flawed morality of the 'us too' argument is transparent. If the demand that 'queers want what straights have got' is taken to its logical conclusion, we would end up campaigning for gay membership of the Ku Klux Klan and neo-Nazi groups like the British National Party. We would start demanding the right of homosexuals to join the Mafia, Christian fundamentalist sects, drug smuggling cartels and El Salvadorean death squads. Our claim for equal rights and treatment can never be unquestioning. It should always be discerning, based on a recognition that not every aspect of straight society is worthy of emulation.

The Gay Liberation Front, which emerged in the wake of the Stonewall Riots, understood this. GLF decisively rejected integrationist strategies that involved queers adapting to hetero society. Whereas straights talked about 'the homosexual problem', GLF branded *homophobic society* as the problem. Challenging 'liberal' heterosexuals with their patronizing pleas for 'toleration', and conservative 'hom-o-sexuals' who sought nothing more than to invisibly blend into straight society, GLF argued that gay self-respect and emancipation demanded a proud and defiant affirmation of homosexual identity. Moreover, law reform was not enough, a fundamental reorganization of society being required to achieve genuine gay liberation.

GLF's critique of straight culture amounted to more than just denouncing violations of gay civil rights and campaigning for equal treatment. Revolutionary not reformist, it singled out hetero masculinity, with its inclination to aggression and violence, as the number-one-enemy of queers and women. The dissolution of straight male machismo was, it argued, the key to ending homo oppression. In other words, the essence of the GLF strategy for queer emancipation was changing society, rather than adapting to it. Nothing less than a total cultural revolution was necessary to overturn centuries of male heterosexual domination.

As well as espousing radical social change, GLF eschewed the timid defensiveness of earlier homosexual rights groups. Not only was 'gay just as good as straight', in some respects 'gay leads the way' – especially with regard to the rejection of oppressive straight machismo. Such defiant assertion of the virtues of gay culture signified GLF's opposition to assimilationism and its commitment to revolutionary change: "In our mistaken, placating efforts to be accepted and tolerated, we've too often submitted to the pressures to conform to the straight-jacket of society's rules...It's especially important for gay people to stop copying straights" (*London GLF Manifesto*, 1971).

Sergeant Leonard Matlovich, who joined the US air force in 1963 and was thrown out because he was gay in 1975, symbolizes many of the old-style assimilationist homosexual attitudes that GLF rejected. He was, as such people were described in those days, a 'straight gay'. Not only did he feel guilty about being homosexual and fervently embrace all the values of hetero society, he was a Christian fundamentalist and right-winger to boot. As president of his local Young Republicans, Matlovich campaigned for the far-right candidate in the 1964 presidential elections, Barry Goldwater. A true-blue patriot, he joined the military at the earliest opportunity and volunteered for three tours of duty in Vietnam. In Matlovich's mind, the US was God's 'chosen nation' and Vietnam was a 'divine war' to assert America's 'global destiny'.

As lesbians and gays rioted in 1969 at the Stonewall Inn to demand an end to victimization, Matlovich, then a self-loathing homosexual, was busily victimizing the people of Vietnam. Working in a support role in the USAF, he was part of the most massive bombing campaign in world history (the US dropped twice as many bombs on Vietnam as it dropped in all operational theatres during the whole of the Second World War). Because he had no recognition of his own oppression as a gay man, perhaps not surprisingly Matlovich did not recognize the oppression he and his military comrades were inflicting upon the Vietnamese. Nor did he see any contradiction between being gay and supporting right-wing, homophobic politics.

Although Matlovich showed admirable courage and determination in fighting the military ban once thrown out of the USAF, it is hard to have much sympathy for someone who so uncritically endorsed straight society and so readily inflicted suffering on others. Far from being a gay role model and a symbol of the struggle for gay freedom, Matlovich and other military homosexuals which the lesbian and gay establishment now parade as heroes and heroines, represent the dark side of queer collusion with hetero society.

The contrast between Matlovich and the early gay liberationists could not be greater. As part of its challenge to the straight consensus, and its critique of hetero institutions, GLF saw the military as the embodiment of society's most oppressive values: hierarchy, domination, violence, prejudice, conservatism, inequality, conformity, authoritarianism.

These military values are not compatible with human liberation in any form, least of all queer freedom. In contrast, anti-militarist ethics coincide with those of the gay emancipation movement: egalitarianism, solidarity, democracy, cooperation, individuality and liberation. This confluence of values, together with a 'rainbow coalition' political philosophy, persuaded GLF to oppose the American war in Vietnam and the British war in Ireland.

On both sides of the Atlantic, GLF chapters aligned themselves with struggles for national liberation and peace. The dominant theme of the 1971 San Francisco GLF March Against War & Sexism was "Vietnam for the Vietnamese! San Francisco for the gays!". In London the following year, GLF marchers on the 100,000-strong Troops Out demonstration demanded: "Police out of gay bars! Troops out of Ireland!".

This support for the struggles of other radical social movements against oppression was a key plank in gay liberationist politics. While earlier homosexual rights groups had been solely concerned with gay issues, GLF saw gay liberation as part of a broader struggle for human freedom. Lesbian and gay oppression was just one aspect of pervasive social injustice. The experience of being excluded from the privileges of straight society inclined many GLF activists towards an instinctive solidarity with others suffering marginalization, especially women and black people. "GLF is a part of the wider movement aiming to abolish all forms of social oppression. It will work to ally itself with other oppressed groups" (*Come Together*, the London GLF newspaper, No. 2, December 1970). In March 1971, *Come Together* No. 5 elaborated this approach: "We are starting to work alongside women, black people, and now those sections of youth and the working class who see the importance of *our* demands as well as their own, to break the old society which puts us all down and to build a new one on the basis of all our needs".

This sense of a shared ethical responsibility for the emancipation both of ourselves and of others contrasts sharply with the 'us-first' gay activism of the 1990s. With few exceptions, lesbian and gay campaigners are now more or less exclusively preoccupied with their own narrow homosexual equality agenda. Given that few straight organizations bother to defend queer interests, it is understandable that lesbians and gay men should concentrate primarily on homosexual issues. What is so disturbing however, about the lack of solidarity with other emancipation movements is that it signifies a basic contentment with the existing social order. Most gay organizations aim no further than winning reforms within the parameters of a society fashioned for the straight majority. GLF's high ideals and its inspired vision of what society could be has been abandoned. Aspirations for a truly liberated queer future have been levelled downwards to the lowest common denominator. Pragmatism, expediency, assimilation and conformity are the bywords of contemporary gay politics.

This new homosexual conservatism is epitomized by drill sergeant Miriam Ben-Shalom, a US army reservist discharged in 1976 because of her lesbianism. Fiercely patriotic, with an unquestioning faith in the virtues of the American system and the US role in policing the world, she fought her dismissal all the way to the Supreme Court, without success. In 1990 she founded the Gay, Lesbian & Bisexual Veterans of America to challenge the military ban. Later that year, as the US started to mobilize for its invasion of the Gulf, Ben-Shalom wrote to President Bush to urge the establishment of a lesbian and gay battalion: "We are willing to go and serve where we are needed, even to the front lines in the Persian Gulf. Mr President, let us show we can do the job with honour, dignity and responsibility". Despite her desperate stars-and-stripes loyalty, Ben-Shalom never received a reply from the President. Even when lesbians and gay men conform rigorously to all the values of straight society and exhibit extravagant patriotism, they are, it seems, still viewed with contempt. Identification with heterosexual institutions does not bring respect, not even a letter of acknowledgement!

Ben-Shalom's ingratiating response to US plans for the invasion of the Gulf contrasts with the anti-war defiance of queer activists. As Britain and the US prepared for war in late 1990, members of ACT UP and OutRage! joined over 100,000 people as they marched through London to demand "No Blood For Oil" and for UN economic sanctions against Iraq to be given time to work.

More than any other social institution, the military is the apogee of heterosexual male power. It is based on the values of aggression and violence. These values are the antithesis of the queer male desire to love men rather than kill them. They are also the cause of much suffering to women, which is why lesbians are glad (and lucky) that they have no need to relate sexually and emotionally to straight men. GLF was right. There is a fundamental contradiction between the machismo of the armed forces and the ideals of lesbian and gay liberation. Since military values and practises are inconsistent with queer freedom, every self-respecting lesbian and gay man has a moral obligation to refuse military service.

two

A Symbol Of Straight Male Culture

The armed forces are the symbol *par excellence* of a straight male culture which exalts toughness, rivalry and aggression. They manipulate, intensify and marshall the brutishness of heterosexual masculinity to create an institution dedicated to cold-blooded and systematic killing. Moreover, the military exemplifies an extreme form of homophobia, with an official ban on lesbians and gays and a *de facto* toleration of queer-baiting and bullying.

The notion that any self-respecting queer would want to copy the flawed example of straight machismo is bad enough. But the idea of lesbians and gays choosing to be a part of the most aggressive and homophobic institution of straight society is beyond belief. Furthermore, our experience of prejudice and queer-bashing ought to instil a hatred of violence and a compassion for the suffering of others, making us disinclined to militarism and war. A higher set of ethical values, including a commitment to resolve problems by non-violent means should, given our own victimization, be axiomatic for lesbians and gay men.

Above all else, it is the explicit, zealous homophobia of the armed forces which makes anti-militarism a logical and moral imperative for queers. In their bid to exclude and root out homosexuals, the services go to obsessive and sinister lengths. Firm evidence of homosexuality is not required. Anyone who does not fit the straight military stereotype can fall under suspicion. A servicewoman who is not sufficiently feminine or refuses the advances of one-too-many male colleagues might find herself targeted for investigation.

Methods include phone-tapping, locker searches, call-tracing, mail interception, covert filming, sexual entrapment and bugging bedrooms. Suspects are liable to be trailed during their off-duty hours, clandestinely photographed, and their civilian contacts investigated.

If the evidence gathered in these ways is not strong enough, a 'suspect' soldier may be arrested by military police (usually in an early morning raid) and be subjected to many hours, or even days, of interrogation. Using psychological intimidation techniques similar to those applied in the investigation of serious crimes, this interrogation can include threats of physical violence, 'outing' to family members, accusations of being in league with enemy agents, and trumped-up charges of sexual assault. Sometimes, the person under investigation is held in solitary confinement or ordered to undertake a punishing schedule of dirty and repetitive tasks (like cleaning the showers and toilets with a tooth brush) in a bid to break their spirit and force a confession. Intimate body inspections are not uncommon. Searches of lockers and personal possessions are invariably undertaken by officers wearing rubber gloves – on the absurd assumption that all queers have HIV and that the virus can be contracted by handling personal effects like diaries and address books.

If a serviceman or woman admits to being gay, that's not enough. They are normally required to reveal every minute detail about their sex life and name all their partners. Refusal can bring additional charges for obstructing a military investigation. To get them to name other homosexual personnel, the arrestee is blackmailed with the lure of a reduced sentence.

The often perverse depths to which the US armed forces will sink, and the frequently tragic consequences that result from its witch-hunts, are dramatically exposed in Randy Shilts' *Conduct Unbecoming: Gays & Lesbians In*

The US Military. For example:

• 24-year-old sailor at the Pearl Harbour Naval Station, Shelli Hurd, was put under three months continuous surveillance. Naval agents secretly photographed her playing sport with friends, coming out of a gay bar, and at her apartment complex.

• First Lieutenant Steve Marose was court-martialled on charges of consensual sodomy and "conduct unbecoming an officer" (for going to a gay club and having an enlisted room-mate). He served nearly 16 months in prison.

• a board of inquiry recommended that Captain Judy Meade of Camp Le Jeune be dismissed from the navy for "engaging in a public association and longterm friendship with a known lesbian...being in the presence or occupying the same dwelling with enlisted marines whom Captain Meade suspected to be lesbians (and) associating with lesbians, thereby giving the perception that she herself was a lesbian, which bought discredit to herself".

• Corporal Valaine Bode, who won the coveted title of Marine Corps Sportswomen of the Year in 1987, heard she was under investigation. Unable to bear the thought of interrogations and dishonour, she sealed her garage door, turned on her car engine, and died shortly afterwards from carbon monoxide poisoning.

The anti-gay purges in the British military are no different. They take their cue from official government policy which states that "both homosexual activity and orientation are incompatible with service in the armed forces":

• a woman sailor was investigated when her name was discovered in the address book of another woman who was under suspicion. Her telephone was tapped and her mail opened. She was abused as a "poof" and a "dyke", and was followed by investigators whenever she went off-base.

• Paul Crone, of the Royal Highland Fusiliers, was imprisoned and tortured after he was seen talking to a gay ex-soldier while socializing off-duty. To make him 'confess', they deprived him of sleep, spat in his food and pummelled him with high-pressure water jets. Beaten while forced to do physical jerks, he had to endure soldiers standing on his back wearing boots with metal studs which cut into his flesh. According to a friend: "For over a week he couldn't wear a shirt without the blood seeping through". Faced with constant violent abuse, Crone admitted his gayness and was dismissed from the forces.

• a member of the Parachute Regiment with 19 years service, Robert Ely, was arrested on suspicion of homosexuality after a private letter was discovered by military investigators. He was held incommunicado for five days and placed under 24-hour surveillance. During the interrogations, he was more or less accused of having sex with his brother and his dog. Not only was he chucked out of the army, Ely also lost his pension rights after nearly two decades of service.

Given these vicious anti-gay witch-hunts, how can any sane homosexual want to join the armed forces? When those who are already enlisted realize they are gay, why do so many fail to initiate steps to get themselves out of an institution that so clearly abhors queers?

At one level, we are bound to feel solidarity with fellow lesbians and gays who are persecuted by the military. But at another level, it is hard to sympathize with closet queers who collude with a homophobic military system. They know the rules have been made by bigots. When they get caught and dismissed they can hardly plead ignorance or surprise. It's self-evident that the military ban on lesbians and gays is oppressive and that no queer with any sense of dignity and pride should have anything to do with the armed forces.

Beyond the arrests, inquisitions, jailings and dismissals, the anti-gay ethos of the armed forces, and the link between hetero masculinity and militarism, is also evident in more subtle ways.

The armed forces are the acme of straight masculinity. Military values are rooted in the bellicose demeanour of straight men. This is not to say that belligerence is an inevitable, biologically-determined feature of male heterosexuality. On the contrary, it is a consequence of conditioning: the ways in which young boys are reared to be rough and tough, and to despise the 'sissiness' of being gentle or tender (which becomes connected in the popular mind with male homosexuality). This early fostering and sanctioning of male aggression, and its association with straight men, is reinforced by the cultural images and icons of masculinity and heterosexuality. They link being a 'real man' with opposite-sex attraction. A rugged masculinity is projected as part and parcel of the socially-prized state of male heterosexuality. This inevitably marginalizes and devalues the queer male identity, with its ostensible lack of 'proper' masculine values.

Straight males tend to be those men who have been successfully socialized into a more aggressive, domineering mode of masculinity, whereas gay men are usually the ones who have not. Queers deviate from the masculine norm in that they are generally (but not always) less fully masculinized than their straight counterparts. It is our 'unmasculine' attributes and failure to 'act like men' that makes us gay men less inclined to violence and aggression.

The fear of being labelled queer can be part of the reason some straight men adopt an extreme form of machismo. They deliberately choose to be unruly, loud and tough as a way of asserting their heterosexuality and distancing themselves from any taint or suspicion of queerness. Hypermasculinity is projected as a signifier of straightness to distinguish a 'real man' from the homosexual 'other'. The flawed reasoning of these lumpen straights is: "I can't be queer, I'm tough". This exaltation of an exaggerated aggressive masculinity by hetero males can lead to violent socially-destructive behaviour such as mugging, rape, vandalism, domestic battery, racist terror and queer-bashing.

The whole ethos of military training and warfare is based on a harsh masculine mentality which is overwhelmingly found among young straight men. Exemplifying all the negative, violent elements of heterosexual male culture, the armed forces cannot be fully understood without first understanding how they mirror the ideas and behaviour which are intrinsic to straight machismo, and how machismo is socially manufactured in a way which links it indelibly to male heterosexuality.

Any cursory examination of social violence reveals that it is primarily heterosexual males who revel in brutalism. While not all straight men are thugs, nearly all thugs are straight men. They are the ones who go on the rampage assaulting women, vandalizing apartment blocks, robbing the elderly and getting into drunken brawls.

It's virtually unheard of for gay men to participate in such violent, anti-social behaviour. Queers prefer to fuck men rather than fight them.

While most people walking alone late at night would feel threatened by the approach of a loud, boisterous group of young straight males, noone ever feels endangered at the sight of several obviously gay men coming towards them in similar circumstances. This speaks volumes about the social menace of male heterosexuality. Just ask anyone who they would prefer as a neighbour: a polite well-behaved gay man or a unkempt straight lager lout. Some homosexuals may well be sissies but, unlike hetero machismo, a bit of effeminacy harms noone. Indeed, it is our refusal to 'behave like a man' that makes us queers less prone to macho aggression.

This is why the 'liberal' argument in favour of gay assimilation into straight society is profoundly stupid. Assimilation involves a minority integrating into the majority culture on terms dictated by that majority. In the case of homosexuals, assimilation means the social acceptance of queers on the condition that they conform to hetero values. However, it's crazy to want gay men to act like straight men. That would result in more vandalism and loutishness. Instead, it is in society's interest for male heterosexuals to behave *more like queers*, the vast majority of whom reject macho violence.

Just ask any police officer about the difference between gay bars and straight bars. Most will report there are rarely any fights in homo venues, but often punch-ups in hetero ones. Likewise it is entirely exceptional for queers to slash bus seats, riot on football terraces, burn down community centres, or graffitti subway trains. Such yobbish behaviour doesn't appeal to us.

While the vast majority of heterosexual men are socialized in ways which predispose them to a hard masculine personality (suited to the military and warfare), a minority end up less rugged. Likewise, although nearly all gay men rebel against machismo, a small proportion (usually straight-identified queers) behave just as belligerently as their heterosexual counterparts. Nevertheless, these few exceptions prove the general rule: straight men tend to be more aggressive than gay men.

On the extremely rare occasions when gay men are involved in acts of violence, it's often because prejudice and stereotypes make those individuals feel unable to accept their homosexuality and lead them to fear being emasculated by it. Queer participation in hooliganism is thus usually a deluded attempt by closet homos to convince themselves of their hetero masculinity, as well as being a ruse to distract the suspicions of their friends. In such circumstances, they are not acting true to their own queer nature, but responding to social pressures to be straight by copy-cating the belligerence of heterosexual men. Moreover, the occasional thuggish gay man is usually the self-hating type who, although he has homo desires, is dominated by a straight mentality.

Most queer men are in contrast unaggressive, tender and empathetic. That's why straight women love our company. We are a pleasant relief from the rough, domineering and boorish behaviour of many (not all) husbands and boyfriends. Women don't like all that macho nonsense, and neither do gay men. However, if pressured, threatened or provoked, we gays can lash out too. But machismo is not instinctive queer behaviour. We have to make a conscious effort to overcome our reluctance to resort to violence, unlike straight youths who are quick to look for trouble.

In these senses, heterosexual men are often a major social liability, whereas most queers are a real social asset. Compared to straights, we're not so desperate to conform to masculine stereotypes. Less afraid to express our feelings, we tend to be more in touch with our emotions. This gives many of us a creativity and sensitivity which has enabled queers to play a disproportionate role in the arts and in professions such as teaching, nursing and counselling. Whether consciously or not, gay men redefine what it means to be a man. We show that masculinity need not be based on uncouthness and machismo.

This is not to say there aren't also plenty of gay men in masculine jobs like coal-mining, lorry-driving and brick-laying. But even in these butch occupations, queers tend to lack the hard-edged, hyper-masculinity of their straight colleagues. Likewise, when homosexuals appropriate the macho drag of body-builders, soldiers and construction workers as a fashion statement, they transform these symbols of straight masculinity by discarding their coarse, aggressive connotations. Queer masculinity embodies the eroticism of maleness without the menace of heterosexual machismo. It is the triumph of style over pathology.

Can any socially-aware person doubt that our society would be an infinitely more pleasant, cultured place to live with fewer heterosexual men around? There'd be vastly less racial violence, gang warfare, wife-beating and late-night brawling. With an increased proportion of gay men, society would be a lot more calm and peaceful, not to mention caring and creative. This homosexualization of male culture is, quite obviously, in the public interest.

The domination and aggression which is such a common feature of heterosexual masculinity, especially among young men, is a central aspect of military culture. The nature and purpose of the armed forces attracts a particular type of recruit. Military training fosters and and accentuates a predisposition to masculine violence, thereby also conferring it with social legitimacy, even honour. It is in essence a system for organizing and professionalizing machismo in the service of the state.

The military's unwritten training philosophy is: to make a soldier, you have to make a man; before you can make a man, you have to break the individual. There is no military necessity for the extraordinary amount of time new recruits spend on drill, square-bashing, the bulling of kit, and barrack room spit-and-polish. The sole purpose of these mind-numbing tasks is to destroy all individuality and create a regimented, blindly-obedient soldier who will instantly follow the most irrational commands without regard to the morality of an order or to their own personal safety.

The uniform is also part of this process of obliteratiing difference and independence. In the words of an ex-soldier: "One of the reasons you wear a uniform is not just so you can look the same, but so you can act the same, and think the same and be the same. That's what the army wants. Uniform people".

Simultaneous with breaking the individual, the military works on 'turning boys into men'. As the armed forces see it, becoming a man requires being subjected to a regime of extreme harshness, bordering on barbarism. Abusive drill sergeants, punishing training schedules, and sadistic initiation rituals are all intended to produce the same result – a fierce, tough masculinity suitable for the waging of war.

It's hardly surprising that the brutalizing process of transforming raw recruits into proficient killers often has a downside and gets out of control. In recent years, there have been a stream of press revelations about bullying in the British armed forces. Drill instructors have been disciplined for stinging trainees with nettles, burning their testicles with lighter fluid, squirting shaving cream into their mouths, bashing their bare butts with baseball bats, pouring bootfuls of urine down their throats, shoving broom handles up their arses, tipping rifle oil over their heads, pissing on their faces, wacking their heads with mallets, smearing their genitals with boot polish, and forcing them into baths of urine and excrement.

While there are many reasons for this bullying, one explanation relates quite directly to straight male values. In our culture, hetero men have historically always victimized women and gay men to sustain their social privilege and power. Bullying is thus a recurrent feature of straight maleness down the ages. Nowadays it is implicitly encouraged by the masculine expectations of toughness and competitiveness that men place on each other. This makes bullying almost instinctive to many hetero males, which is why it can so easily flourish in a social institution like the military which puts such a premium on men parading their machismo. Bullying is therefore not accidental. It is a logical consequence of the brutalizing process whereby the military seeks to make 'real men' out of rookie soldiers.

Although not officially endorsed by the armed forces, bullying is tacitly tolerated. This is partly because it is seen as a useful 'freelance' way of creating the belligerence and pecking order that are considered essential in warfare, and partly because it is recognized as an inevitable side-effect of the aggressive military training regime.

Homophobic bullying is a significant aspect of the violent brutality that exists within the armed forces. This has a lot to do with the bellicose straight male values that have traditionally been central to the functioning of the military. But there is an added reason too. In most armies, the sponsoring of homophobia is deemed necessary in order to contain and repress the homoerotic impulses which are a sub-text to military life and a sub-conscious motivation to success in warfare. The bonding between soldiers working in their predominantly single-sex units – where they shower, work, eat and sleep together – has strong queer undertones. When men or women depend on each other in life and death situations and are required to risk their lives for the sake of their comrades, it is not surprising that feelings of intense loyalty and affection can easily develop. And this is the rub. The military needs homoeroticism to function, but despises it because the 'softness' and 'tenderness' of queer desire is seen as undermining the aggression and bloodlust necessary for warfare. Hence the traditional discrimination against homosexuals by the armed forces and the tacit toleration of anti-queer hatred.

Moreover, the homoeroticism of the military is often tinged with misogyny. Given that the integration of men and women in the armed forces is still fairly limited, and that most personnel spend the majority of their time in predominantly single-sex situations, no man joins the military if he likes women. Spending lots of time on military exercises with 'the guys' is part of army routine. It's not compatible with married life or opportunities for sex with women. Indeed, this separation of the sexes, and the chance to mix mainly with male 'buddies', is precisely what makes military life so attractive to many of the men who enlist.

One way of containing and repressing these ever-present, unconscious queer undercurrents is the military's unofficial green light to bullying and initiation rituals which have a two-edged frisson of male homoeroticism and homosadism. These express same-sex desire in the displaced, socially-acceptable form of sexual cruelty. Typical macho 'pranks' include a gang of soldiers stripping new recruits naked, shaving off their pubic hair, and rubbing scouring powder, after-shave or chemical solvents into their genitals. Other initiation ceremonies have been known to include sodomizing trainees with rifle barrels and flogging naked squaddies tied to beds or flag-poles. At the sub-conscious level, the function of these barbaric practices is the suppression of queer longings by associating them with acts of humiliation and degradation.

Military organization revolves around the core values of domination, hierarchy, authoritarianism and conformity. These are overwhelmingly the values of straight men, not gay men or women. Based on a hierarchy of rank and the conquest of enemies, the military system mirrors the way heterosexual males have historically subordinated women and gay men. The authoritarian pattern of men as unquestioned heads of families and rulers of nations, together with the demand that each gender conforms to its own designated masculine and feminine roles, is the means by which straight males have traditionally sustained their social power and privilege over female and queer 'inferiors'. This use of expectations, rules and punishments as methods of subjection and control is also part of the *modus operandi* of the military. In other words, there is a basic confluence of values and methods between male heterosexuality and the armed forces. The military is the creation of straight men and it reflects their mentality and behaviour.

This is not to say that homosexuals are incapable of domination and conquest and cannot excel on the battlefield. After all some of the greatest commanders in history have been lovers of men, including Alexander The Great, Julius Caesar, Richard The Lionheart, and one of the founders of the US army, General Steuben, who played a major role in winning the American War of Independence. In this century, homosexuals and bisexuals can be counted among Britain's most prominent military leaders: Field Marshalls Kitchener, Haig and Montgomery, and Admiral Mountbatten.

Queer militarists are, however, exceptions. The vast majority of gay men are not attracted to macho aggression and warfare. Furthermore, these 'gay' military commanders, and their antecedents in the 'armies of lovers' in ancient Greece, were not gay in the sense that we understand it. None of them defined themselves as gay or dissented in any way, apart from having sex with men, from dominant straight male values. Even the 'queer' armies of Sparta were wholly hetero-identified. They existed within a misogynistic, slave-owning culture where heterosexuality and straight marriage were socially dominant and same-sex love affairs were strictly subordinate.

The notion of homosexuals as a separate class of people, and the existence of a distinct gay sub-culture, only began to develop very slowly from the seventeenth century. This meant that men who had sex with men prior to this time had no reference point other than straight male culture and therefore, not surprisingly, internalized all its macho values. Indeed, until the last quarter of the twentieth century, even in large western cities the vast majority of queers were hetero-identified and many still are, including those who emulate straight masculinity and join the military. They may have gay sex, but they have no independent gay identity. They are acting out, and conforming to, straight expectations of how men should behave.

In contrast, the new generation of self-identified queers, which refuses to live life on terms dictated by the heterosexual majority, is far more critical of straight male values. Although some may wear military fatigues, it's all style and subterfuge. Their play and parody with the paraphernalia of war is not a sign of support for militarism. Indeed, a strong, independent queer identity seems to be consonant with the explicit rejection of masculine brutality.

It is not just the violent nature of the armed forces which contradicts the culture and interests of the lesbian and gay community. The military ethos of anti-individualism and conformity is the antithesis of queerness. It is our sexual difference, and our *right* to be different, which is central to queer identity and emancipation. The rigid hierarchy and authoritarianism of the armed forces pushes everyone into a predetermined place and role. It demands unquestioning obedience. These military values negate the precious right to choice which allows us the freedom to explore and express our queer desires. Psychoanalytic

At a deep unconscious level, there is a fundamental difference between the psyches of heterosexual males and queer men. This originates from our different objects of sexual desire. Straight men tend to see other men as sexual rivals, competing with them for the carnal conquest of women. This makes it very difficult for them to feel anything other than a superficial camaraderie with fellow males. In the absence of feelings of genuine brotherhood unmitigated by sexual competitiveness, straight men have fewer qualms about hurting other males, and this makes them more amenable to waging war. Homo desire, in contrast, inclines gay men towards compassion and solidarity with members of their own sex. Although there is an element of sexual rivalry in queer culture in that gay men compete with other men for sexual partners, this competitiveness is moderated by the fact that every male rival is also a potential lover. Because other males are possible objects of desire, gay men are less well disposed to harming them and therefore disinclined to warfare. This, then, is the deep sub-conscious explanation for the psychic differences in homo and hetero attitudes towards violence and war: straight men are more prone to fight men, whereas gay men are more likely to love them. That's what makes sex and love between men so subversive.

Lesbianism is threatening in a different way. Military culture embodies the macho straight male values of conquest and domination. Just as heterosexual men subordinate women, the military subjugates 'the enemy'. The misogynistic male impluse to hegemonize women thus coincides with the domineering temperament necessary for warfare. This relatedness between the militarist and misogynistic mentalities is evident in the way rape is frequently perpetuated by conquering armies. Lesbianism challenges these psychic processes and thereby threatens the macho ideology on which the military is based. Refusing to be dominated by men, women who love women make heterosexual men feel inadequate and vulnerable by refusing to submit to the power of the prick. Indeed, at an erotic and emotional level, they dispense with men altogether. For many straight males, this is their greatest fear. To lose their control over women undermines their male identity and masculinity, shattering egos and self-confidence. Such men are no good in battle, which is one reason why lesbians have been so zealously witch-hunted out of the armed forces.

three

Assimilation Is Not Emancipation

Jess Jessop wanted to be a real man. He hated being queer. Plagued by guilt and the fear that friends might discover his secret, Jess resolved to prove his manhood. No-one would dare call him faggot if he went to war and risked his life for his country. And that is what he did. As Randy Shilts explains in *Conduct Unbecoming*, Jess volunteered for service in Vietnam in a frontline US Marine unit. During the war, he showed extraordinary bravery under fire. But he was not motivated by courage at all. He was driven by a reckless, suicidal bravado. Under suspicion as a 'sexual deviant', Jess wanted to be killed to atone for the shame he felt about his homosexuality. Rather than live with the disgrace of being queer, he preferred to die a heroic, manly death. That way, nobody would ever taunt him again.

Jessop was not the only soldier who felt this way. In the pre-Stonewall era, many gay men were deeply troubled by their homosexuality. They imbibed the straight hate which said queers were inferior, criminal, sick, perverted and immoral. Service in Vietnam was a way out. As Randy Shilts recalls: "Leonard (Matlovich) hoped that the military orderliness would enable him to overcome his homosexuality. He had read that it was just a phase people went through and outgrew, and he figured the quickest way to outgrow it, to prove his manhood, was to go to war". There were other gay men who felt even worse about their sexuality. "Some resolved it would be better not to live than face the collective revulsion of an entire culture. And some went to Vietnam just for that reason: to die".

There are, of course, many different reasons why lesbian and gay people enlist in the military: to escape unemployment, acquire technical skills, get away from home, or fund a college education. However, for gay men who are insecure about their masculinity and disturbed by their homosexuality, military service is often about proving their manliness and thereby disproving their queerness. Randy Shilts sums up their simplistic, self-deluding syllogism thus: "Soldiers are real men. Queers are not real men. Therefore a soldier cannot be a queer".

This warped logic leads many gay people who depise their sexuality to sign up for military service in the hope that the tough, macho life of soldiering will block out their homosexual longings and turn them straight. It drives some to acts of extreme heroism in battle in a desperate attempt to compensate for the shame they feel about their homosexuality. This bravery is motivated by more than a desire to protect comrades and secure victory. It is also a way of winning the respect they feel is being denied to them because of their queerness.

This was the motivation for Armistead Maupin's service in Vietnam. Now one of the most celebrated modern gay writers, he was then wracked with angst about his homosexuality. In a bid to overcome his feelings of shame and prove he was a real man, Maupin enlisted for Vietnam. His deliberate choice of a naval combat assignment was a bid to surmount the insecurities he felt about his masculinity and to win the social admiration which he felt his gayness was undermining.

As well as being desperate to prove their manliness, many gay men like Maupin who join the military are super-patriots (as are many lesbian servicewomen). They conflate loyalty to one's gender role with loyalty to one's country. This may be part of the same psychic defence mechanism. Many of these individuals have internalized homophobic attitudes. They believe being gay is 'abnormal'. Ashamed of their deviance and terrified by the social rejection it threatens, they want to be the same as straights and win their approval. They go out of their way to be ultra-conformist and conservative in every other respect of their lives. Often both a mask for their homosexuality, and an attempt to compensate for what they see as dishonourable same-sex desires, this humiliating quest for acceptance by straights sometimes includes a zealous, ostentatious commitment to establishment politics and fervent patriotism.

This was certainly the case with Private Pete "Spike" Smith (his name has been altered slightly at his request). For many British soldiers, a posting to northern Ireland at the height of 'The Troubles' was hardly a welcome prospect. However, being couped up in fortified barracks, working extra long hours, and patrolling the menacing streets of Belfast in the 1980s was not, in Smith's eyes, all bad. It kept him away from his "city of temptation", London, where he might succumb to the homosexual urges he was trying to suppress. Smith identified with all things straight. Totally closeted, he wanted to blend in. His greatest wish was to be just like the other guys. Dating girls, getting married, having children. For him heterosexuality was the good life, the right life. He wanted his share of it. Smith also convinced himself that soldiering in Belfast would get rid of 'the demon' of male attraction that was 'ruining' his life. It was a chance to prove his manhood in the service of 'Queen and Country'. Born to a working-class family in London, Smith adored the monarchy and looked back with nostalgia to the hey-day of the British Empire. It is not hard to see his obsequious loyalty to traditional values as a compensation for his violation of those values in his furtive, guilt-ridden, anonymous gay encounters in parks and public toilets.

On the other side of the Atlantic, Midshipman Joseph Steffan shared Smith's true-blue sentiments. He had the background, looks, grades and values of an all-American boy. Hiding his sexual secret out of sight, Steffan went on to become one of the top trainees at the US Naval Academy at Annapolis. Probably the proudest moment of his life was in December 1985, when he sang 'The Star Spangled Banner' in President Reagan's presence at the army-versus-navy football game. He may have been gay, but Steffan was a loyal, patriotic American to the core.

Smith and Steffan are not untypical. They represent a particular type of assimilationist homosexual. To serve in the armed forces involves conforming to the rules of a homophobic, hetero institution. Demanding more than merely blending in, it requires *collusion* with a military system that discriminates against us. To be complicit with this institution necessitates a certain mind-set. That is why lesbian and gay soldiers are invariably straight-thinking, straight-acting queers. Infatuated with straight culture, these 'hetero homos' want to be like straight people and to be liked by them. Possessed of a slave-like, hetero-loving mentality, they are psychologically dependent on straight society for their values and for their sense of self-worth (or their lack of it). Becoming a soldier is, for them, becoming part of a 'distinguished' and 'respected' straight institution. It is a way to recapture the self-esteem and social approval which they believe homosexuality has denied them. They enthusiastically embrace the straight culture of the armed forces precisely because it embodies the social norms of heterosexuality and machismo which they look up to. These people are heterosexualized homosexuals. They 'fit in' with the armed forces because military culture is all about the obliteration of difference and they are happy to comply with a conformist culture that aims to create uniform, regimented, straight-acting people. To be 'the same' as heterosexuals is their most cherished aspiration.

But why should lesbians and gay men mimic straight culture and seek self-validation on the terms laid down by hetero norms and institutions? As the Gay Liberation Front argued a quarter of a century ago, and as modern queer activists proclaim today, our liberation lies in proudly celebrating our sexual difference and in winning the social acceptance of our own distinctive and virtuous queer values. Merging imperceptibly into the straight majority and getting asborbed into its institutions is a sure-fire strategy for the loss of homo identity and the annihilation of queer culture.

In contrast to the fawning homosexual apologia of the past, nowadays no self-respecting lesbian or gay man can base their claim for human rights on the argument that homosexuals are 'just the same' as heterosexuals, or that queers are 'just as good' as straights. The mere fact of our existence as human beings should be quite enough to entitle us to human rights, without any need for justification or pleading. In any case, the denial of difference is profoundly dishonest. There *are* differences between straights and queers. We are *not* all the same. While some lesbians and gay men do mindlessly ape heterosexual values, many do not. The sexual behaviour, relationships, aesthetics, and lifestyles of even conservative gays (let alone queer dissidents) are quite dissimilar from those of the average heterosexual. That's not something we should deny.

In many ways, this transcending of heterosexual mores is a positive and immensely liberating experience. William Masters and Virginia Johnson studied straight and queer couples, documenting their research findings in *Homosexuality in Perspective*. They found that compared to most straights, queers (especially lesbians) tend to be more sexually adventurous, with a wider repertoire of sexual stimulation. On average our sex acts last longer and result in a higher level of erotic satisfaction. There is more egalitarianism and mutuality between homosexual partners. Other research has found that we're less bound by the strictures of traditional morality and more experimental in relationship patterns. There's no need for a marriage certificate to validate our sense of commitment to each other, and we've adapted much better to safer sex. In all these senses, the fact that homosexuals are different from heterosexuals is a real virtue that we should all be proud to shout about. This is not to say, of course, that queers are superior to heteros. But in certain respect we do perhaps lead the way and could teach straights a thing or two. Sometimes, homo is *bettero*. We should never hold back from proclaiming the positive differences.

Furthermore, to be different is a fundamental human right. The acceptance of sexual pluralism and diversity is just as much a sign of a mature democracy as is the acceptance of racial difference. The denial of the right to be different, as in the institutionalized homophobic discrimination of the military, is profoundly authoritarian. When the armed forces intrude into people's private lives and attempt to exclude and punish those who do not conform to heterosexuality, it is taking away one of the most precious individual freedoms – the right to sexual difference.

Lesbian and gay people, because of our different sexuality and lifestyle, also help make a more heterogeneous and interesting society. That's a good thing. There is nothing great about social homogeneity. It is boring and results in social sclerosis. In contrast, the celebration of difference, including sexual difference, is a force for social innovation and renewal. It enlivens and enriches our whole culture.

One of the many valuable aspects of being queer is that it gives us the opportunity to develop a critical attitude towards the traditional, and often unquestioned, values of mainstream society. From scepticism new understanding and insights evolve. This is the motor for social progress. In maintaining an anti-assimilationist, autonomous queer identity, we are thus safeguarding our independence from the dominant straight culture. This is not only good for our own psychological esteem and well-being, it also helps sustain a sub-cultural 'deviance' which is essential to engender social and cultural change. The sexual transformation of society has the potential to benefit *both* gays and straights. In that sense the queer refusal to conform to hetero expectations is of much wider social worth.

From the perspective of valuing sexual difference, homo conformity and assimilation is anathema. The integrationist strategy of the homosexual establishment assumes that lesbian and gay freedom is about queers adapting to, and being accepted by, straight society. It involves homosexuals conforming to heterosexual laws and values. That's not liberation – it's capitulation! And it doesn't win us respect or human rights either.

Lieutenant Elaine Chambers of the Royal Army Nursing Corps found that out the hard way. She was a model soldier. Very discreet about her sexuality, she conformed in every way to straight expectations. But her record and respectability didn't help her one iota when she came under suspicion of being lesbian. Military investigators took apart her private quarters and subjected her to marathon interrogations of fifteen and nine hours. She was treated with all the harshness that might be meted out to a saboteur or spy. They even tried to pin charges of sexual assault on her, which drove Chambers to contemplate suicide. Within three months she was dismissed from the British army, damn lucky not to have been court-martialled and imprisoned. So much for the idea that blending quietly into straight society affords protection.

Irrespective of how badly the armed forces mistreat homosexuals, there is a more fundamental question that needs answering. Why would queers want to join a straight institution and conform to straight expectations? Is heterosexuality really so great? What about the alarming rates of divorce, rape, wife-battery and child sex abuse within heterosexual families? Can anyone honestly say that straight life is better? Happier? More fulfilling? For some maybe. But many of us would not wish the hetero hell of marriage, 2.4 children and a mortgage in suburbia on our worst enemies. Moreover, as the London Gay Liberation Front newspaper asked: "Do we really want to be integrated with a society we regard as sick? Do you really want to be accepted by so-called normal people? On whose terms?" (*Come Together*, No. 4, February 1971). This recognition of the often ugly reality of straight society suggests that queer emancipation is not contingent on us adapting to the heterosexual status quo, but on us radically changing it. The problem in society is homophobia, not queer deviance and dissent.

Winning law reform and equality with straights has its limitations. Usually it means little more than homo conformity with hetero society. *We* comply with *their* system. It is parity on heterosexual terms – equal rights within a framework determined and dominated by straights. Our worth should be measured on *our* terms, as opposed to the criteria laid down by heteros. Allowing the values and choices of queers to be judged by heterosexual society, based on its traditions and norms, is an invitation to permanent rejection and exclusion.

Ultimately, assimilationism is just another means whereby heterosexuals continue to call the shots. It obliterates any distinctive queer identity and culture, creating homosexual versions of heterosexual lifestyle and morality. Assimilationism means us giving up the unique and enriching aspects of our own lesbian and gay experience. It requires our surrender to heterosexual norms. Absorbed and invisibilized, we become mere facsimiles of heterosexuals.

What an assimilationist strategy implies is that the lesbian and gay experience embodies nothing worthwhile, innovative or liberating. It suggests that queers have nothing positive to contribute to society, nothing that straights can learn from or benefit from. That attitude is as much nonsense as it is insulting. We *have* got something positive to offer. There are lots of queer insights that can contribute to the enrichment of heterosexuals and the betterment of society. Compared with most straight people, for example, lesbians and gay men are more willing to transgress the boundaries of traditional masculinity and femininity. As a result, gay men tend to be less macho than straight males, which means fewer crimes of violence and vandalism. Because lesbians are usually less reliant on men than their hetero sisters, this greater independence and assertiveness has enabled them to make a pioneering contribution to women's advancement in previously all-male occupations.

What finally clinches the case against assimilationism is the fact that it has not succeeded in securing dignity and human rights for lesbians and gays. Being deferential and straight-acting hasn't saved queers from job discrimination and queer-bashing violence. Nowhere is this more evident than in the armed forces.

Colonel Margarethe Cammermeyer blended in perfectly. A model of American womanhood, she was no 'bulldyke'. Her career was impeccable, from volunteering for Vietnam to winning the Bronze Star. After leaving the army, she joined the reserves. In 1985, they named her Nurse of the Year and soon afterwards she was appointed head of nursing in the Washington National Guard. Four years later, when up for consideration for the plum job of Chief Nurse of the National Guard throughout the whole US, she told the truth about her lesbianism in response to a routine security clearance check. That was the end of her military career. Twenty-eight years of patriotic loyalty and distinguished service counted for nothing. Despite proving she was the best, and otherwise conforming to every expectation the military had of her, Cammermeyer was ousted.

A similar fate befell Captain Paul Starr, the youngest US Air Force Squadron Commander in Europe. He was highly respected and respectable, being the perfect discreet gay man who passed for straight. Moreover, Starr excelled at his job, winning a string of military awards, including Strategic Air Command Administrator of the Year. However, on discovery of his homosexuality, this was no protection. Summarily court-martialled, he was sentenced to 18 months imprisonment for consensual sodomy in private and for fraternization with an enlisted man. The ultimate insult was that Starr was forced to serve his time locked up in a cell in Fort Leavenworth, Kansas, together with murderers and rapists. That's what happens to nice assimilationist homosexuals. They still get fucked over by straight society.

Thinking straight and acting straight is not enough. The homophobes won't get off our backs until we *are* straight. If we are not prepared to renounce our queerness, we have to look to effective, lasting ways to ensure our emancipation from hetero intolerence. Long ago, the Gay Liberation Front realized that tinkering with the straight system doesn't work. It has to be fundamentally transformed: "Legal reform and education against prejudice, though possible and necessary, cannot be a permanent solution. While existing social structures remain, social prejudice and overt repression can always re-emerge...We should not confuse legal changes with real structural change. Legality can always at some point be changed to illegality" (*Come Together*, No. 2, December 1970).

What this means is that genuine queer liberation involves more than mere law reform and legal equality. It requires an end to heterosexual hegemony and to all erotic guilt and repression. That necessitates changes in cultural attitudes as well as in social structures and institutions. The ultimate irony is that this strategy for queer liberation leads to sexual liberation for *everyone*. In defending our right to be queer and fighting for queer freedom, we also create the basis for the liberation of heterosexuals from the sex-negative culture in which they too are trapped. The assimilation of queers into the majority straight culture is not just destructive to lesbians and gay men. It is also indirectly against the interests of heterosexuals. Mere equalization of the law invariably means equality on terms predefined by a puritanical, straight-dominated legislature. This perpetuates the anti-sex status quo, which hurts heteros as well as homos. Everyone would therefore benefit from the realization of the more sexually enlightened cuture that queer activists are striving to achieve.

The modern queer agenda is post-equality. It's geared to a wholesale renegotiation of sexual values and laws. We want more than simply an equal age of consent for heterosexuals and homosexuals, and more than mere equal treatment in the way other laws, such as those against prostitution and pornography, are enforced. The *whole* system has to change. That demands social transformation. It means, in the words of the Gay Liberation Front, moving "beyond civil libertarian goals" to achieve a "revolutionary change" which "abolishes the gender system" and creates a "new social order" which is not based on "straight male privilege":

> The gender-role system is the root of our oppression ...We are taught there are certain attributes that are 'feminine' and others that are 'masculine'...By our very existence as gay people we challenge these roles...homosexuals don't fit into the stereotypes of masculine and feminine, and this is one of the main reasons we become the object of suspicion...

Freedom for gay people will never be permanently
won until everyone is freed from sexist role-playing.

(*London GLF Manifesto*, 1971)

These ideas, which reject shallow reformism, are as per-
ceptive, relevant, challenging and inspiring today as they
were in the early 1970s. The linchpin of queer liberation
remains the same: a thorough-going cultural revolution to
break down the gender system that demands men and
women conform to rigid masculine and feminine roles and
dictates the way we are supposed to think and act, including the social expectation of heterosexuality. This system
pressures men into the masculine role of domination and
aggression and women into the feminine role of subordi-
nation and passivity. Queer persecution is a direct result
of our failure to conform to the gender roles expected of
men and women. Most gay men are deemed incompletely
masculinized and we fail to fulfil the male role of sexually-
possessing and subordinating women. In contrast to heterosexual women, lesbians are less feminized and
dependent on men, and they refuse to make themselves
available for male sexual conquest and the servicing of
men's domestic needs. This social demand for conformity
to gender roles and expectations denies choice, crushes
individuality, and sustains homophobia and misogyny. It is
the ultimate reason for our second-class status and the
number one obstacle to our emancipation.

The military is the incarnation of the gender system and
the ultimate defender of that system. Its whole ethos is
based on the straight male machismo which oppresses
women and queers. This machismo is a direct result of the
gender division of labour which assigns to men the social
task of specializing in domination and violence. The most
extreme and brutal expression of this masculine violence
and domination is warfare.

The armed forces are an institutional expression of the
straight male-dominated gender system. They are part of
the problem. So what is the solution? Merging into
straight society and tinkering with the status quo won't
resolve the essentially homophobic nature of the dominant

culture. Only when the whole gender system is changed fundamentally, together with all the social institutions which sustain it, will we be able to achieve the truly emancipatory objective of ending heterosexual supremacism.

Regrettably, most lesbian and gay organizations have nowadays turned their backs on these radical ideas of GLF, reverting to a pre-Stonewall quest for social respectability and acceptance on heterosexual terms. They are, by and large, shorttermist, accommodationist and reformist.

This hegemony of homo conservatism is all the more depressing because there is a profound need, for the sake of the collective well-being of the queer community and for the ultimate betterment of all humanity, to resurrect the defiance and imagination which fired the early gay liberationists.

GLF and its recent successors, like OutRage! in Britain and Queer Nation in the US, have been movements with an inspired vision of what society could become. Although motivated by a spirited idealism, their dream of a sexually emancipated society is nevertheless rooted in practical possibilities. We, the human species, have an extraordinary capacity for self-critical reflection and reasoning. This enables us to make a conscious choice to reject our present restrictive conditions of existence and transform them into something more empowering and liberating. Now, more than ever, we need to make our queer dreams come true.

four

Why Defend Straight Society?

In late 1990, as the US began its military mobilization for the Gulf War, the gay lobby group, the National Gay and Lesbian Task Force, came out in opposition to American intervention. Highlighting the billions of dollars being poured into the military build-up, it pointed out that just one week's spending on preparations for the war was greater than all the money spent on AIDS research over the previous decade.

This is not the only example of society's perverted priorities. When have political leaders ever bothered to declare war on the homo hatred that is wrecking our lives? Why are so few public funds available for lesbian and gay helplines which can reduce teenage suicides? What is stopping the police from mounting a concerted campaign against the queer-bashing violence that maims thousands of homosexuals? These questions demand answers. We know the government has the power and resources to alleviate many of the hardships faced by lesbian and gay people, but it refuses to take the necessary action. So long as the state sanctions homophobia, no queer should lift even a finger to defend straight society.

What have straights ever done for queers? They have given us centuries of torment and violent persecution. The anti-queer hatred of straight people has led to us being stoned to death in Antiquity, burnt alive in the Middle Ages, hung from gallows during the Age of Empire, and incarcerated in mental asylums for much of this century. Right up to the 1970s, in so-called civilized democracies, lesbian and gay people were being chemically castrated and given electric-shock aversion therapy to cure their 'perversion'. Rarely has any social evil rivalled the barbarism of the straight crimes against queer humanity.

And it isn't over yet. Iran and Saudi Arabia retain and enforce the death penalty for homosexuality. In Mexico and Brazil, right-wing death squads hunt down and execute faggots. While the state-sanctioned murder of homosexuals no longer exists in the West, queer-bashing attacks are still rife in 'democratic' countries and legal discrimination remains systematic. For all the advances of the last two decades, there is not a single nation on this planet where queers have full legal equality with straights. Even the most enlightened countries, like Denmark and Sweden, discriminate against lesbian and gay people in terms of the right to adopt children and access to donor insemination services.

The legal systems of supposedly 'advanced democracies', such as Britain and the United States, are systems of sexual apartheid. They subject lesbians and gay men to separate and unequal treatment in terms of the laws governing sexual relations, marriage, employment and so on. This institutional discrimination is premised on the doctrine of straight supremacism: the idea that heterosexuals are superior to homosexuals. Reflecting this belief, western law denies lesbian and gay people many of the basic human rights that straights take for granted. This entrenched denial of legal rights to queers is in some ways analagous to the race discrimination practised by the former Apartheid regime in South Africa. While obviously not based on the extreme economic deprivation and police state brutality that characterized the South African system, there are marked parallels at the level of supremacist ideology and legal discrimination.

Lesbians and gay men in the West have never, of course, been banned from living in particular neighbourhoods, as were black people under Apartheid. Yet we can be refused housing by a landlord who is prejudiced against our homosexuality, and in only a handful of countries and cities do we have any kind of legal redress against such discrimination.

Nor are queers officially forbidden to use 'hetero only' bars or restaurants. But in most countries we can be lawfully refused service by any retail outlet which objects to 'poofs' and 'dykes', and there is nothing we can do about it.

Although queers are not excluded from the right to vote, which is what Apartheid did to black people, we might as well be. Queer votes count for little in electorates dominated by straights and in legislatures with a in-built hetero majority which consistently refuses to uphold lesbian and gay human rights.

In some respects, the system of sexual apartheid causes forms of suffering that even the South African regime never inflicted. Black people under Apartheid may have been denied the right to inter-racial marriage and separated from their partners by the mining and domestic labour systems – but they were never subject to a *blanket ban* on marriage and refused inheritance rights on the death of their partner, as happens to lesbians and gay men in nearly every country of the world.

Moreover, although black families in South Africa were often torn apart by the economics of the Apartheid system, black children who lived with their parents could expect love, understanding and support, and a sense of self-respect and racial pride. In contrast, gay kids grow up in the prison of a heterosexual home, with straight parents who often despise, mistreat and reject them. This leaves many of us suffering from a lack of identity and low self-esteem, which can later lead to severe depression and destructive behaviour patterns such as alcoholism and attempted suicide.

Given the physical and mental violence that the system of sexual apartheid inflicts upon queers, how can we be expected to feel any sense of obligation or loyalty to straight society? Why should we spill a single drop of queer blood to defend a homophobic state which treats us as second-class citizens? Since we are denied human rights, surely noone can expect us to risk our lives defending a country that victimizes us?

These truths may seem self-evident to any queer with intelligence, confidence and pride. Yet many homosexuals continue to enlist in the military to defend the straight state. What they see as service is in fact servility to a system that treats us as inferiors. Respectability is mistaken for respect. Patriotism is confused with pride.

Defence of one's country is, alas, also the defence of a homophobic legal system which robs queers of all dignity. The military defends the state and sustains its power. Since the government is homophobic, part of what the armed forces are defending is that homophobia. By acting as the guarantor of the security of the state, the armed forces thereby also act to guarantee straight privilege. They protect the nation, including all its heterosexist institutions. The military is thus not only anti-gay in its own policies, it defends the whole system of sexual apartheid.

Aside from the question of whether we should be complicit with the homophobia of any straight institution, the armed forces are particularly cynical and manipulative in their treatment of queers. When it suits them to look the other way, lesbians and gays are unofficially allowed to serve. This often happens during periods of national emergency, such as the wars against Japan and Germany from 1939-45. When the Allied Powers were perilously threatened, the military suddenly became far less interested in rooting out faggots and dykes. In both the US and British armed forces there were attempts to 'rehabilitate' men caught in homosexual acts, particularly if they were deemed to be 'normal' young men for whom gay sex was a 'momentary aberration'. These 'reclaimables' were either sent to a psychiatrist or punished with hard labour to 'toughen them up'. Afterwards, providing there was no evidence that they were 'incorrigible degenerates' or 'habitual sodomites', they would often be reassigned to new units. However, these more relaxed attitudes were a passing phase. Once the imminent threat from Germany and Japan receded, the policy was tightened up again – at least for a while. Then, during the final push for the liberation of Europe in early 1945, when maximum troop levels were needed, the US Secretary of War ordered the reinduction of previously discharged homosexuals who had not committed sex acts during active service. This renewed enlightenment didn't last long either. As soon as victory was won, the purges recommenced. Thousands of queers who had previously been regarded as war heroes were dismissed or court-martialled and imprisoned.

Overall, an estimated two million lesbian, gay and bisexual people enlisted in the British and American forces during the Second World War. Accounting for about ten percent of military strength, they made a significant contribution to the liberation of fascist-occupied Europe and Asia. Nevertheless, although queer soldiers, sailors and aircrews fought just as hard as anyone else for freedom, it was a freedom they were never allowed to share. They returned to 'democracies' where homosexuality was still totally illegal. In Britain, it was not until 22 years after 1945 that the freedom queer soldiers had fought for was partly extended to their own lives with the limited decriminalization of male homosexuality. As an added insult to those lesbians and gay men who had risked their lives defending freedom against fascism, this reform excluded members of the armed forces. Likewise in the US. Fifty years after the end of the Second World War, gay sex is still unlawful in nearly half the states of the Union and open homosexuals continue to be barred from the military.

Somewhat hypocritically, the US armed forces have always accepted lesbians and gay men whenever it is expedient to do so. Homo bodies are suddenly no longer reviled when there's a wartime crisis and a shortage of military personnel. Prior to the Korean War, for example, the US navy dismissed an average of 1000 gay sailors every year. In 1950, when the fighting was fiercest, the discharges fell to 483. But the year the peace settlement was

Why Defend Straight Society?

39

brokered at Panmunjom – 1953 – the number of homosexuals ousted from the navy rocketed to 1353.

The same story was repeated in Vietnam. The first big build-up of American forces began in 1965-66. Because there was an urgent need to boost the military intake, from that time onwards draft boards only rejected conscripts who could 'prove' their homosexuality. Later, when the success of the Communist Tet Offensive in 1968 pushed the American forces to breaking point, the boards unofficially accepted all but the most overt and effeminate gay draftees. These changes in policy are reflected in the navy discharge figures. Each year from 1963-66, which was the less intense phase of the war, the US navy sacked more than 1600 lesbian and gay personnel. By 1969, as the American forces were under seige and desperate to boost their combat strength, the discharges dropped to 643. Queers were cynically used as cannon-fodder to sustain an unjust and unpopular war. Queer lives are expendable.

And it happened all over again during the 1991 Gulf War. Petty Officer Phil Zimmerman was one of several top-notch Arabic linguists who were witch-hunted out of the navy for being gay in the 1980s. As the Gulf War loomed, the military was caught with too few Arab-speaking personnel. Desperate to make up numbers, National Security Agency officials attempted to reenlist the gay translators it had previously purged from the services.

This about-turn was part of wider policy reversal adopted by the Pentagon to fulfil Gulf mobilization quotas. The aim of the Stop Loss policy was to maximize military personnel levels for the forthcoming war by minimizing discharges. In November 1990, the Secretary of the US Army ordered an end to the release of personnel in all but the most exceptional circumstances. This paved the way for thousands of lesbians and gay men, many of them open about their homosexuality, to be sent to fight in Operation Desert Storm.

The sudden liberalization of military regulations was hinted at by Lieutenant Commander Ken Satterfield of the US

Army Reserves. He told the *San Francisco Chronicle* that discharge proceedings against lesbian and gay soldiers may be "deferred" until after the war, depending on the "operational considerations" of individual units. "Just because a person says they're gay doesn't mean they can stop packing their bags", he said. In other words, military chiefs were quite happy to enlist queers when it suited them and to discharge queers when it didn't.

This was indeed the experience of US army reservist Donna Lynn Jackson. Her open lesbianism posed 'no problem' to service in the Gulf War. She was duly assigned to the 129th Evacuation Hospital in Saudi Arabia. Unbeknown to Jackson, the army was planning to use her in the war and discharge her when it was over.

Similar double-standards were shown by the British forces during their moblization for the Gulf War. A prominent gay rights activist, Julian Corlett, who was also a reservist in the Royal Army Medical Corps, was sent call-up papers in late 1990. On reporting to his unit, he was surprised to be told that his homosexuality was not considered a bar to military service. "My homosexuality wasn't a problem", said Corlett. "They told me they weren't interested in my private life". A spokesman for the North-Eastern District Army Command, which covers Corlett's home town, confirmed the sudden switch in policy towards gays in the military: "Homosexuality on army property is not tolerated, but what a person does in his own spare time is obviously his own business". Non-plussed by revelations that Corlett was Chair of the Scunthorpe Gay Men & Women's Group, the spokesman merely stressed that he would be expected to give up his campaigning for gay rights if he was posted to the Gulf. However, as soon as the case got national publicity, the military hastily backtracked. Corlett was suddenly notified that a recent illness disqualified him for overseas service.

The relaxation of the military's anti-gay ban was confirmed by a still-serving soldier who told *Capital Gay* newspaper in London: "During the Gulf War, I knew lots of medics who were called up and they told the call-up board 'Look

41

I've been out of the army three years and I'm now gay'. The board told them that didn't disqualify them, or that they would 'overlook' it; and so these gay men served during the war". Within months of the conflict ending, this soldier confirmed that the purges of queers had resumed: "Now the war's over and they want cuts, gay men and lesbians are being slung out left, right and centre". It was, of course, a cheap way to get the redundancies demanded by the scaling down of the defence budget. Dumping soldiers because they're homos means there's no need to give them severance pay or full pensions. The US military adopted the same policy. According to the *Wall Street Journal* an estimated 700 gay soldiers who fought in the Gulf War were facing dismissal because of their homosexuality in mid-1991, even though many of their commanders knew they were gay before they were posted to fight in Operation Desert Storm.

To straight society queer lives are worth nothing. General Norman Schwarzkopf, the American commander in the Gulf War, described homosexuality as "incompatible with military service" because, he said, it impairs good order, discipline and morale. However, if faggots are so 'unsuited for military service', why the fuck did the US armed forces call-up so many perverts for duty in the Gulf? It seems that queers are expected to put their lives on the line for their country, but their country is unwilling to ensure human rights for its queer citizens. While homosexuals can die in the national interest, it is apparently not in the national interest to give homosexuals fair and equal treatment. How readily our rulers turn morality on its head. Straight society treats a soldier who kills the enemy as a hero, but condemns the soldier who loves someone of the same sex as unfit for service. Faced with such bigotry, queers have no obligation to defend a sick, straight society. Indeed we have a moral duty to fight it.

five

Forces Of Subjection & Oppression

Onward queer soldiers. Kill! Kill! Kill! In 1991, an estimated 50,000 lesbian and gay military personnel joined Operation Desert Storm, the one-sided slaughter in the Gulf that left 200,000 Iraqis dead, most of them civilians, for the loss of a mere 234 Allied soldiers. The war was not about the defence of democracy or human rights. After all, the 'liberation' of Kuwait restored the feudal dictatorship and the West has subsequently given Iraq a free hand to massacre the Kurds. The prime motive of the Allied invasion was to maintain western control of cheap, accessible oil supplies. "Our position should be the protection of the oilfields", said Les Aspin, Chair of the US Armed Services Committee.

One US fighter pilot described the sorties over Iraq as follows: "It's almost like you flipped on the kitchen light at night and the cockroaches start scurrying, and we're killing them". That's what happened on the road to Basra. Thousands of retreating Iraqi soldiers, plus civilians fleeing the fighting, were helplessly trapped in flat, open country. Unlike cockroaches, they had no where to run or hide. Making not the slightest effort to secure their surrender, the US air force bombed and strafed without mercy, turning 40 miles of road into an open crematorium littered with charred corpses. Simultaneously, they reduced Iraq's second city, Basra, to rubble with 'surgical precision' air strikes destroying apartment blocks, schools, hospitals, shops, cinemas and other key 'strategic' targets. Even when the Iraqis were able to run and hide, they didn't stand a chance. Over 400 died when a US missile blew apart a 'military command and control centre' which turned out to be a civilian airraid shelter.

The Gay, Lesbian & Bisexual Veterans of America wanted to participate in this indiscriminate slaughter, and even offered to raise a battalion of homosexual volunteers. Moreover, lesbian and gay soldiers who joined the blood-letting in the Gulf are now hailed by many homosexual rights groups as heroes and heroines of the struggle for equality. Their loyalty to the straight state and its war objectives is deemed a virtue. It's presented as evidence that queers are worthy of human rights, as if we only deserve equality providing we can prove our unquestion-ing patriotism and loyalty to hetero society.

It is hard to comprehend that members of the gay commu-nity, which has suffered such immense discrimination, can so readily cooperate in the victimization of other people. The waging of indiscriminate war is perhaps the ultimate victimization and the ultimate denial of freedom. What right have we got to demand our freedom if we are not pre-pared to support the freedom of those who are likewise subjugated?

Sadly, queer collusion with the oppression of other people is not something new. In 1954 it wasn't US bombs that rained down on the villages of northern Vietnam but mil-lions of leaflets. They were part of a US propaganda offen-sive, code-named Operation Virgin Mary, designed to turn the catholic population against the communists (who had, ironically, been America's allies in the war against Japan). In hysterical, ominous tones the leaflets urged villagers to flee south to the American-backed regime in southern Vietnam: "Beware! The Virgin Mary has fled south. Follow her or be slaughtered by the barbarian communists".

Lieutenant Tom Dooley of the US Navy joined this propa-ganda offensive, feeding the world's media fictitious tales of the Viet Minh tearing out the tongues of catholic priests, disembowelling women, and jamming chopsticks in children's ears to stop them hearing the word of God.

But Dooley also carried the secret burden of being a self-hating gay man. To compensate for the shame he felt about his homosexuality, he sought to win respect by embracing a super-patriotism, which led him to lie in the name of defending the interests of the United States and vanquishing its enemies. He did the bidding of the straight military with gustso. Hailed as an American hero, this gay serviceman's shameless propaganda helped to create the climate of anti-communist hysteria which led to the US invasion of Vietnam.

The American war policy was to bomb northern Vietnam back to the Stone Age. Three million Vietnamese were killed and four million made homeless refugees. Eight million acres were rendered sterile wastelands by chemical defoliants, leading to mass starvation. Hundreds of thousands were interned as political prisoners by the pro-American dictatorship in southern Vietnam, and at least 50,000 opponents of the dictatorship were assassinated under the US-backed Phoenix Programme.

Second-lieutenant Margarethe Cammermeyer had no objections to service in this genocidal war. She volunteered for Vietnam. Although she never killed anyone, she was part of a military machine that murdered many. Now, since she has come out as a lesbian and fought the ban on gays in the military, Cammermeyer is portrayed as a role-model by the homosexual establishment. Their attitude seems to be that it doesn't matter what suffering she helped inflict on the people of Vietnam. All that matters is that she is a lesbian, and all lesbians deserve our unquestioning support and loyalty. Do they? Even those who have acted in support of dictatorial regimes and unjust wars?

Whenever the established order has been threatened, the armed forces have helped suppress the civilian population and thwart popular movements for social change. This has happened even quite recently in Britain and the United States. All throughout the 1960s, the US National Guard was used to put down the black rebellions against racial injustice in cities like Detroit and Los Angeles. Troops were also deployed to quash student protests against the war in Vietnam, with four anti-war demonstrators being shot dead at Kent State University in 1970.

British soldiers have acted similarily, playing a major role breaking strikes by the firefighters and municipal employees during 1977-78, and brutally suppressing the Irish Republican movement in the north of Ireland. In 1972, the Parachute Regiment murdered 13 peaceful protesters in Londonderry, shooting most of them in the back. Ten civilians (half of them children) were killed, and hundreds maimed, by soldiers firing rubber and plastic bullets between 1972 and 1981. Following claims of widespread army brutality against Republican sympathisers, the British government was forced to set up an inquiry. The Compton Committee concluded that electric shocks, hooding, loud noise, and sleep and light deprivation had been used by the security forces and that these methods constituted "physical ill-treatment". The European Commission On Human Rights was even stronger in its condemnation, declaring that the British army was guilty of "torture, inhuman and degrading treatment".

There is nothing worthy or honourable about lesbians and gay men wanting to serve in an institution which has been involved in these acts of civil repression. Having homosexuals in the ranks doesn't alter the fundamentally undemocratic and repressive nature of the military. It is no consolation to those on the receiving end of military abuses that the perpetrators are lesbian or gay. Yet by demanding unquestioningly the right of homosexuals to serve in the armed forces, many gay rights organizations are effectively demanding the right of queers to participate in acts of brutality and slaughter. This may not be their intention, but it *is* the consequence of their largely uncritical, sycophantic attitude towards the military.

It is ironic that although the armed forces supposedly exist to defend our democratic way of life, they are arguably the most undemocratic institutions in our society. Military personnel are arbitrarily denied many of the fundamental freedoms they are entrusted to defend. This has grave social dangers. The more soldiers are deprived of freedom themselves, the more readily they will act to deny freedom to others. This authoritarian streak has lead some sections of the British armed forces to consider mounting a *coup d'état*.

During the political crisis surrounding the 1974 miners' strike, some military chiefs were alarmed by the power of the unions and feared the election of a left-wing Labour administration. Field Marshal Lord Carver has since confirmed that "fairly senior" officers had suggested that if the "extreme Left" pushed for power "the army would have to do something about it".

Likewise, the Labour Party's commitment to a non-nuclear defence policy in the early 1980s sent shock waves through the military establishment. In 1981, top brass drew up contingency plans in the event of a Labour government coming to power. These involved petitioning the Queen to sack a Labour government if it attempted to implement a policy of unilateral nuclear disarmament.

Moreover the military is committed to a counter-insurgency role to suppress the civilian population in periods of 'civil emergency'. The British army's official *Land Operations Manual* defines the state's enemies as not only "guerrillas" and "terrorists", but even mere "dissidents". The subversion which the military exists to counter is described as "action taken to undermine the military, economic, psychological, moral or political strength of a nation and the loyalty of the subjects".

The section of the *Manual* detailing the army's internal security role sets out its function as anti-terrorism, peacekeeping and "dealing with civil disturbances resulting from labour disputes, racial and religious antagonism and tension or social unrest". Citing the types of disturbances that the army might need to take action against, the *Manual* lists "unlawful assemblies, strikes and picketing, civil disobedience, riots, arson and looting".

Given our own experience of persecution, it is strangely perverse that any queer would agree to be part of a military system which is prepared to use violence to protect oppressive governments against legitimate demands for social justice at home and abroad. Our involvement in the military system helps deny to others the liberation we demand for ourselves.

The struggle for queer freedom can never justify our collusion with institutions that refuse freedom to other persecuted communities and nations. Nor can it exonerate us from moral culpability when we are complicit in the suffering of those persecuted peoples. Since we expect solidarity from others in our struggle for lesbian and gay human rights, we should be prepared to reciprocate that solidarity by refusing all cooperation with a military machine that defends injustice and suppresses freedom.

The Duty To Refuse Military Service

Edward Carpenter, the nineteenth-century gay Utopian socialist and advocate of homosexual rights, believed that queers had a destiny beyond mere adaptation to, and acceptance by, straight society. Far from encouraging the view that lesbians and gay men are just the same as straights and that they should aspire to conform to hetero society, Carpenter saw queers as a unique and special class of people, which he called Uranians. They were different from straights and that difference should not be erased, but protected and treasured. He argued that the generally greater sensitivity and tenderness of gay men compared to straight men is a social asset because it repels queers from violence and warfare towards creative and caring endeavours, that benefit all of society. Writing in *The Intermediate Sex*, Carpenter suggested:

> It is possible that the Uranian spirit may lead to something like a general enthusiasm of Humanity, and that the Uranian people may be destined to form the advance guard of that great movement which will one day transform the common life by substituting the bond of personal affection and compassion for the monetary, legal and other external ties which now control and confine society.

Uranians had the potential, Carpenter argued in *My Days and Dreams*, to lead society forward "in the direction of Art and Human Compassion". The essence of Carpenter's argument is that the greater peaceableness of most homosexual men gives them the potential to help make a kinder, gentler culture. Instead of seeking to conform to the aggression and violence of straight institutions like the armed forces, queers should be proud of their non-belligerence and demand that hetero institutions renounce their destructive machismo.

This idea that queers have a special role to play in the creation of a new, more enlightened social order was revived by the gay liberation movement of the early 1970s with its defiant assertion that 'gay shows the way':

> In some ways we are already more advanced than straight people. We are already outside the family and we have already, in part at least, rejected the 'masculine' and 'feminine' roles society has designed for us. In a society dominated by sexist culture it is very difficult, if not impossible, for heterosexual men and women to escape their rigid gender-role structuring and the roles of oppressor and oppressed. But gay men don't need to oppress women in order to fulfil their own psychosexual needs, and gay women don't have to relate sexually to the male oppressor, so that at this moment in time, the freest and most equal relationships are most likely to be between homosexuals.
>
> (*London GLF Manifesto*, 1971)

There is, of course, nothing intrinsically superior about homos compared to heteros. However, in some respects, as Edward Carpenter and the GLF foresaw, queers are, or could be, the pioneers of a more humane civilization. We have the potential to transcend the oppressive limitations of heterosexual culture. Since we have that precious potential, it would be foolish to reject it in favour of a dull, unquestioning conformity to macho straight values and institutions.

Being marginalized by society as 'outsiders' and 'deviants' ought to give us queers a more critical perspective on all social institutions, including the military. Instead of blithely assuming that everything straight is wonderful, we should be inclined to a healthy scepticism towards straight culture.

No hetero institution is more deserving of our scepticism than the military. It denies democratic rights to its own members, tolerates bullying, lacks mechanisms for public scrutiny and accountability, discriminates against lesbians and gay men (and women and racial minorities), and has been used frequently to suppress popular movements for social justice and national liberation in countries like Ireland and Vietnam.

Above all else, the military is a straight institution. It is organized by and dominated by the hetero majority. The purpose of the military is the defence of a society ruled by straights. It serves straight interests and upholds the macho straight values of violence and homophobia. Everything about the military is inimical to queer freedom.

Moreover, the military is an instrument of state power. The state is homophobic, enforcing legal discrimination against lesbian and gay people. As a part of the repressive apparatus of the state, the armed forces embody this anti-gay discrimination, banning queers from joining the military and forcing out those it discovers within its ranks. In defending the state, the military also defends the anti-queer repression of the state.

Lesbians and gay men have a right, and even a reponsibility, to refuse allegiance to a homophobic government and its homophobic military apparatus. Faced with unjust laws that discriminate against homosexuals, queers are duty-bound to deny legitimacy to the (straight) governing elite and to withdraw all consent and cooperation from governmental institutions such as the armed forces.

According to liberal theory, rights carry with them responsibilities. But in the absence of civil and human rights, the duty of reciprocal responsibilities ceases to exist. This means that we queers are under no obligation to join the military to protect those who refuse to protect us. Instead, we have a duty to withhold our loyalty from the institutions of a homophobic state, such as the armed forces, and to do everything in our power to subvert and sabotage the straight system that treats us as second-class citizens. You don't have to be a queer revolutionary to realise this, just a homo with a bit of common sense and self-respect.

Don Slater was no 1960s radical. In fact, he was rather conservative. But even Slater was incensed that the US military was privately drafting queers for Vietnam while publicly proclaiming a ban on homosexuals. In 1968, his campaign group, the Committee To Fight Exclusion Of Homosexuals From The Armed Forces, began placing adverts in the alternative press with the following message: "Every homosexual has a right and a duty to refuse induction (into the military)". Slater argued that so long as the military endorsed discrimination, gay men had a moral obligation to resist the draft.

This idea of queer non-compliance with homophobic institutions like the military is rooted in the civil disobedience tradition of Mahatma Gandhi and Martin Luther King. Unjust laws must be broken, not obeyed. Those who deny human rights forfeit all legitimacy and loyalty. Resistance to oppression is an ethical duty. These ideas are just as relevant today for lesbians and gay men as they were in the past for the Indian independence movement and the US black civil rights struggle.

Private James Darkin joined the Corps of Drums of the British Army soon after his sixteenth birthday. What he thought would be the start of an exciting military career, turned into two years of "living hell". Taunted as a "queer", Darkin was on various occasions dipped in a duckpond, kicked, forcibly bathed, urinated over and scrubbed down with scouring powder. His pubic hair was shaved off and his clothes were smeared with boot polish. According to his brother, Darkin made repeated complaints to senior ranks but they took no action. Indeed, one officer admonished him to "stand up and be a man". Eventually, with no means of getting redress against the intolerable, constant bullying, Darkin curled up in his bunk and took a massive overdose of painkillers, which killed his pain forever.

Private Darkin's tragic suicide was able to happen because the authoritarian structure of the military gives soldiers very restricted, inadequate mechanisms for the resolution of grievances. Service personnel have few legal rights. There is no independent watchdog. When the military is largely a law unto itself, abuses are bound to take place and sometimes queers are the victims.

The armed forces do not respect our civil rights. Why, then, should we enlist and serve? Is there any reason for queers to give a damn about the fate of the straight state? How can anyone seriously suggest that we have an obligation to defend the phoney democratic system that denies us equality? Don't we have moral right to subvert and destroy the hetero institutions that hold us down?

Collusion with a homophobic state and a homophobic military is collusion with anti-gay discrimination. What's more, to do the bidding of those who victimize us betrays the cause of queer freedom. That's why all queers everywhere have a duty to refuse collaboration with a homophobic military system that symbolizes the most oppressive aspects of straight male culture: aggression and domination. By contributing to the evolution of a more compassionate civilization transcending violence and war, queer resistance to military machismo can benefit all of humanity.